Holiday Histories

Juneteenth

Denise M. Jordan

Heinemann Library
Chicago, Illinois

HEINEMANN-RAINTREE

TO ORDER:

☎ Phone Customer Service **888-454-2279**

💻 Visit **www.heinemannraintree.com** to browse our catalog and order online.

Editorial: Rebecca Rissman
Design: Kimberly R. Miracle and Tony Miracle
Picture Research: Kathy Creech and Tracy Cummins
Production: Duncan Gilbert

Originated by Chroma Graphics (Overseas) Pte. Ltd
Printed and bound in China by South China Printing Co. Ltd.
The paper used to print this book comes from sustainable resources.s.

ISBN-13: 978-1-4329-1042-6 (hc)
ISBN-10: 1-4329-1042-6 (hc)
ISBN-13: 978-1-4329-1050-1 (pb)
ISBN-10: 1-4329-1050-7 (pb)

12 11 10 09 08
10 9 8 7 6 5 4 3 2 1

Library of Congress Cataloging-in-Publication Data
Jordan, Denise.
  Juneteenth / Denise M. Jordan.
    p. cm. -- (Holiday histories)
Summary: Describes the holiday known as Juneteenth Day, which has roots in Texas and which celebrates the end of slavery in the United States. Includes bibliographical references (p.) and index.
1st Edition ISBNs 1-4034-3505-7 (hc),
1-4034-3690-8 (pb.)
1. Juneteenth--Juvenile literature. 2. Slaves--Emancipation--Texas--Juvenile literature. 3. African Americans--Texas--Galveston--History--Juvenile literature. 4. African Americans--Anniversaries, etc.--Juvenile literature. 5. African Americans--Social life and customs--Juvenile literature. 6. Slaves--Emancipation--United States-- Juvenile literature.
[1.Juneteenth. 2. Slaves--Emancipation. 3. Holidays.]
I.Title. II.Series.
E185.93.T4J67 2003
            394.263--dc21

Acknowledgments
The author and publishers are grateful to the following for permission to reproduce copyright material: **p. 5** ©Getty Images/Yellow Dog Productions; **pp. 6, 7, 11, 12, 15, 18** ©Bettmann/Corbis; **pp. 8, 9, 10, 13, 26** ©Corbis; **pp. 14, 21, 22, 23** ©Hulton Archive/Getty Images; **pp. 16-17** ©Library of Congress; **pp. 19, 20** ©The Granger Collection, N.Y; **p. 24** ©Robert Brenner/PhotoEdit; **p. 25** ©Michael Newman/PhotoEdit; **p. 27** ©Joe Harpring/AP Wide World Photo; **p. 28** ©Joseph Sohm/ChromoSohm Inc./Corbis; **p. 29** ©Bob Daemmrich / PhotoEdit

Cover photograph reproduced with the permission of ©PhotoEdit/Bob Daemmrich

The publishers would like to thank Nancy Harris for her assistance in the preparation of this book.

Every effort has been made to contact copyright holders of any material reproduced in this book. Any omissions will be rectified in subsequent printings if notice is given to the publisher.

Contents

Some words are shown in bold, **like this**. You can find out what they mean by looking in the glossary.

A Celebration of Freedom

The smell of barbecue is strong in the air.

Food covers the picnic tables. Families gather together to celebrate the day of freedom.

Children listen as their elders tell the story of freedom. History is being celebrated. What day is it? It's Juneteenth Day!

What Is Juneteenth Day?

Juneteenth Day is the oldest African-American holiday. It was the very last day of **slavery** in the United States. It was the day all **slaves** learned they were free.

Many slaves were forced to work in cotton fields.

Abraham Lincoln was the President of the United States. He ordered all slaves to be **freed** on January 1, 1863. Slaves in most states heard the news. But the slaves in Texas were not told. They were told on June 19, 1865.

This painting shows Abraham Lincoln reading the Emancipation Proclamation.

Why Were African-Americans Slaves?

Many southern states had large farms called **plantations**. The owners of the large farms needed a lot of workers. They wanted workers they did not have to pay.

This drawing shows slaves being sold. Many families were separated when they were sold to different owners.

Men hired ships and sailed to Africa. They trapped African men, women, and children to take back to America. The Africans were then sold into **slavery**.

An Argument Over Slavery

Fredrick Douglass escaped slavery. He became an abolitionist and a writer.

Some people believed that **slavery** was wrong. Many northern leaders wanted to end slavery. But **plantation** owners did not want to free the **slaves**.

These men are having a meeting about slavery.
Many people wanted to end slavery.

Southern leaders were tired of the northern leaders
telling them to free the slaves. They decided to form
their own government.

A War Is Started

President Abraham Lincoln said the southern states could not form their own government. If they tried, he would send the army to stop them.

These men were part of the Confederate States of America.

The southern states started their own government. They called themselves the Confederate States of America. They formed an army and navy. Then, they attacked the United States and started the Civil War.

Rumors of Freedom

During the **Civil War**, Lincoln put out an order freeing all **slaves**. It was called the **Emancipation Proclamation**. Most slave owners refused to tell their slaves about freedom. But **rumors** of freedom quickly spread throughout the South.

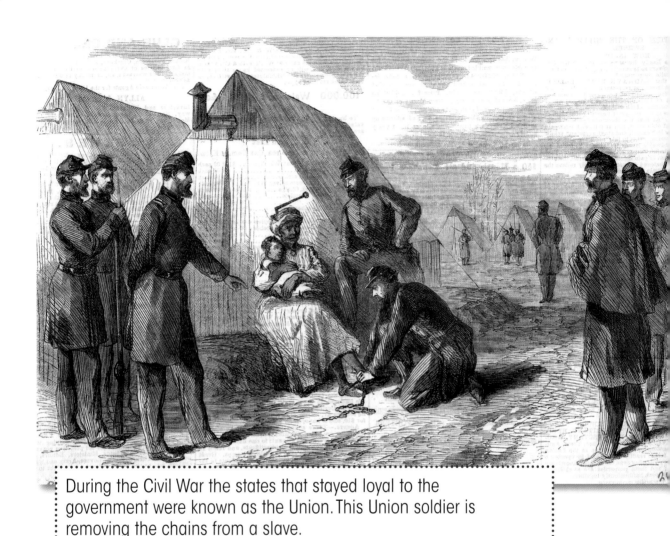

During the Civil War the states that stayed loyal to the government were known as the Union. This Union soldier is removing the chains from a slave.

One person told another, then another, then another. Slaves learned of their freedom by word of mouth. Some slaves left the **plantations** and headed for cities. Some of them went to help the Union soldiers.

The Union Goes to Texas

Slaves in Texas were not told about freedom. The **plantation** owners did not want to lose their slaves. If slaves talked about freedom they were punished.

On April 9, 1865 the Confederate army **surrendered**.
The **Civil War** was over. The Union troops marched
into Texas and brought the news of freedom.

Free at Last

This drawing shows a family of slaves receiving the news of freedom.

On June 19, 1865, Union General Gordon Granger went to Galveston, Texas. He read an order that stated "all **slaves** are free." The news spread quickly.

Some slaves shouted for joy. Others hugged family members, cried silently, or prayed. Many began to celebrate. The long wait was over.

Celebrating Freedom

People everywhere celebrated the end of **slavery**. They brought food and drinks to share. They danced and sang. Children played games.

African-Americans no longer had to fear being sold into slavery. They were no longer forced to work for free. They were no longer considered to be another man's property. They were finally free.

What Does Juneteenth Mean?

In the South, only white children were allowed to go to school. It was against the law to teach **slaves** how to read and write. Some slave owners would punish their slaves if they found out that they could read.

These children were allowed to learn how to read and write.

Since slaves were not allowed to go to school they pronounced some words differently. During all the telling and retelling of the last days of **slavery**, June 19 became Juneteenth.

These children were slaves. It was against the law for them to learn how to read and write.

How Is Juneteenth Celebrated Today?

Many cities like Houston, Dallas, and Fort Worth, Texas, hold big parades. People cheer as colorful floats, marching bands, and community groups go by.

Besides games and food, storytelling is a part of the celebration. Stories are told to remind people about the first days of freedom.

Where Are Juneteenth Celebrations Held?

Early Juneteenth celebrations were held at churches. Some were held in fields in the country. Later, **freed slaves** purchased a park for their Juneteenth celebrations.

Today, Juneteenth celebrations are held in schools, churches, community centers, and city parks. Many people even have small Juneteenth celebrations in their homes.

Juneteenth Jubilee

Most people celebrate Juneteenth Day on June 19. Some celebrate on January 1, the day Lincoln ordered **slaves** to be **freed**. Others celebrate on the day slaves were freed in their state.

Juneteenth Day is not a national holiday. Only eight states have made it a state holiday – Texas, Florida, Oklahoma, Delaware, Alaska, Idaho, Iowa, and California. However, Juneteenth Day is celebrated in many states across the country.

Important Dates

Juneteenth

1860	Abraham Lincoln elected president of the United States
1861	The Civil War begins
1863	The **Emancipation Proclamation** issued by Abraham Lincoln
1865	The Confederacy **surrenders** on April 9; end of the Civil War
1865	**Slavery** ends in the US on June 19
1866	First Juneteenth Day is celebrated in Texas
1872	Freed slaves purchase Emancipation Park in Houston, Texas for Juneteenth celebrations
1892	Freed slaves purchase Booker T. Washington Park, near Mexia, Texas, to hold Juneteenth celebrations
1980	Juneteenth Day becomes a state holiday in Texas
1994	Movement started to make Juneteenth Day a national holiday

Glossary

abolitionist person who speaks out against slavery

Civil War war between the southern and northern states of the United States

Emancipation Proclamation statement signed by President Abraham Lincoln freeing slaves

freed not controlled by someone else.

plantation large farm where crops such as coffee, sugar, or cotton are grown

rumor story told that is passed along from person to person

slave person who works for someone else for no money

slavery practice of owning slaves

surrender give up

Find Out More

Nelson, Michael. *Juneteenth.* Minneapolis: Lerner Books, 2006.

Rosinsky, Natalie M. *Juneteenth.* Minneapolis: Compass Point Books, 2004.

Taylor, Charles A. *Juneteenth A Celebration of Freedom.* Greensboro, NC: Open Hand Publishing, LLC, 2002.

Index